# PAINTING THE SPIRAL STAIRCASE

## ANNE CALDWELL

INDEPENDENT  INNOVATIVE  INTERNATIONAL

Published by Cinnamon Press,
Meirion House,
Tanygrisiau
Blaenau Ffestiniog,
Gwynedd,
LL41 3SU
www.cinnamonpress.com
The right of Anne Caldwell to be identified as author of this work
has been asserted by her in accordance with the Copyright,
Designs and Patent Act, 1988. Copyright © 2016 Anne Caldwell.
ISBN: 978-1-909077-84-3
British Library Cataloguing in Publication Data. A CIP record for
this book can be obtained from the British Library.
Designed and typeset in Palatino by Cinnamon Press. Printed in
Poland. Cover design by Adam Craig
Cinnamon Press is represented in the UK by Inpress Ltd
www.inpressbooks.co.uk and in Wales by the Welsh Books
Council www.cllc.org.uk

# Acknowledgements

*Virgo* – Heavenly Bodies Anthology, Beautiful Dragons Press, 2014, *Raleigh Bikes, 1976* – Spokes, Otley Wordfest Press, 2014, *The Glass Heart* – Blog: http:// rebeccagoss.wordpress.com – (For Children's Heart Week. 2014) *Clocks* – Commended in Poets and Players Competition, Manchester, June 2014, *Slow Train North*, displayed on Hebden Bridge Railway Station, 2013, *Losing the Language, Sunday Morning Chichester Cloisters*, Seductive Harmonies Anthology, Avalanche Press, 2012. *Losing the Language* - published in Live from Worktown Anthology, 2014 - Bolton Poetry Festival, *Waymarker* – Sheffield Midsummer Poetry Festival, Exhibition 2014, and longlisted for the National Poetry Competition 2015. *Seasonal Affective Disorder*, Indent (Staffordshire University Magazine, 2012). *Some Enchanted Evening*, Beehive Poets Anthology 2015

The two sequences in the book featuring Aberdeen and Berlin were commissioned for a festival in Berlin, *After Image*, and first printed as a limited edition art book of 30 copies for the exhibition at the Emerson Gallery, Berlin, 2013 published by *Sources*

Heartfelt thanks to fellow writers/artists:
Andrew Forster, Vicki Feaver, Carola Luther, Rebecca Goss, Char March, Glynis Charlton, James Williams, Amanda Dalton, Jan Fortune, Keith Hutson and Jack Wright.

# Contents

*For Anton*

# Painting the Spiral Staircase

# After Image One

## i. Losing the Language

I roll words I remember like gobstoppers of pure sugar,
or amber beads, each with a trapped creature
longing to flex its wings.

I've a kirk and a kirk-yaird, a herring quine's empty kist,
flooer-beds of roses gardening the streets
of Airberdeen.

I've a view of the dreich sea
from an auld hoose, a winda in a tooer block.
I've one snapshot of my faither

when he was a bairn in a cowboy suit.
That's about the sum of it. At night, I listen
for the murmur of the Caledonian Sleeper.

## ii. The Docks

In 1969, Dad photographed
three submarines moored in the harbour.
Low in the water.

Their crews were smoking roll-ups, winking
at the broad-shouldered girls packing ice crates.
Careless of danger,

a local man in a flannel suit and flat cap
stared hard at their German insignia.
The next day they'd slipped back into the Deep North.

The same space was choked with trawlers.
Dad focused on the herring fleet with his Leica
and a wide-angle lens, his feet slipping on blood and fish guts.

Before Texan drawls and Stetsons,
before the oil rush,
this was his Silver City. The granite love of his life.

### iii. Cranford Terrace, Aberdeen.

It is late afternoon.
Light is rosy, full of juice.

The outhouse. The single garage bolted shut.
Wooden doors painted billiard green.

At the bottom of the garden,
two apple trees where I learnt to walk.

Dad's shoulders confettied with blossom,
Mother in a pale pink twin-set with her arms outstretched.

From the stairwell, the chime
of the Anderson clock my grandfather built.

A church bell calling for its flock. Evensong.

## iv. Blackout

Dad spent hours sprawled on the attic floor,
aged thirteen, in his tank top and grey trousers
with a stash of American magazines.

He listened to news of bombings
filtering up from the crystal set,
borrowed his stepmother's sewing shears

and cut out freight trains, railroad depots,
fighter jets, sweethearts with demi-waves
and pointy breasts.

I know he had a set square, protractor
and metal ruler. Measured an exact
quarter of an inch round every picture.

Already a whizz at maths,
he pasted each lithograph with fish glue,
smoothing them out with a chamois leather

across the hardboard walls. He traced
the dissolving borders of Europe
with an ink-stained finger,

marking countries that had fallen to the Führer.
He stared at that stretch of North Sea
where mariners were rescuing men

like pickpockets working the folds
of an overcoat, slipping
their merchant boats into Norwegian waters.

Half a century later, I discover the attic.
I shut my eyes, listen
for his scissors

slicing paper as U-boats nosed
their way towards the shore
and Aberdeen blacked itself out.

## v. Home City

I walk the Granite Mile towards The Citadel.
The old girl's a little down at heel,
*Esslemount & Mackintosh* all boarded up.
Three ex-fishermen near Shore Brae
are kippered with drink, squatting
on the step of an Irish Pub.

Good Friday. The kirks are empty and the port is quiet.
Boiler-suited figures tend the brigs, trawlers towering
above my head. The place still reeks of fish,
refrigerated wagons all parked up,
the quay swilled down. Here's the *Far Scotia*,
*Maurst Feeder*, and *Suchramada* from Mumbai:

vessels big enough to scrape the seabed clean of life.
The herring's gone, the cod is under threat.
I wonder what my Dad would make of it—
this lack of stewardship and mariners
who've skippered all their lives, ditching most
of their quota over the side?

In the Maritime Museum I find a whale's ear,
an iron harpoon and a walking stick
fashioned from a narwhal tusk. None of this
trawling can bring him back. Yet, as I stand
on the spot he cine-filmed in '65,
I sense him sweating in a woollen suit,

a poly-cotton tie flapping in my face,
his horn-rimmed specs,
a soft-skinned palm in mine:
a man who never had to winch,
or land a catch, or feel his fingers
blistered up by rope and salt.

## vi. I Spy

Here's my boat and concrete train
in the playground, painted green.
Mum's kicked off her Sunday shoes:
paddle, paddle.

I make a drawbridge out of sand,
hear the bell along the beach.
Ice cream's melting down my hands,
drips between two wafer things.

Gran says, *sit still in church,*
*your father's gone to a higher place.*
My muddy knees are sore and scratched
by a cushion with a cross.

The man's voice says I'm a sinner.
but I ate all my carrots today.
I see in the dark and Mum's not happy.
I think dad's hiding in the attic.

I'm a pony locked in a box.
Giddy up! Let me free!
I'll gallop back to grandma's house.
Round and round the apple trees.

## vii. Provost Alexander's Maze

I break in through a hole
in the chain-link fence.
Roman numerals are verdigrised.
There's a burnt patch of earth,
(no bread or wine),
a Smirnoff bottle, used condom,
and a packet of Lambert and Butler
scrunched from someone's fist.
I lose my bearings as the sun goes in.

When I was a kid, this place
was a city, a temple to the art
of getting lost, coppiced hazel
bursting into life, shadows
latticing the tarmac paths.
Every year, I'd rediscover
its heart of granite plinth
and sundial bronzed with light:
time reduced to a line
across a burnished face.

## viii. Aberdeen Art Gallery

*'To help us ensure the comfort and safety of all the visitors to the gallery please do not let children play with the water in the fountain. Thank you.'*

Fiona and I were folded into a bed
with a pot hot-water bottle under a quilt
that remained damp even at the height of June.
There were *butteries* for breakfast. We scrubbed
the bird bath in a garden of gnarled trees
and floribunda roses past their best.

Later, we strolled along Rosemount Viaduct
to the gallery to stare at carcasses
by Francis Bacon. I sniggered until reprimanded,
felt the chill of granite pillars against my cheek,
then hopscotched across a chequered floor
as red paint dripped down the canvases.

At midnight, Gran's stairwell clock began to strike.
Lumps of butchered meat and howls
of conscripts filled the bedroom
as I felt for my sister's spine.
I pressed my feet against hers until the sun rose
and traffic hummed along Anderson Drive.

## ix. Pastures New

*A painting by James Guthrie — Aberdeen Art Gallery*

Guthrie paints a farmer's girl and gives her grace:
his ten-year-old queen-o'-the-fields, herding her geese
across the flatlands, hat pulled low, hair tied with a scrap of cloth.
Her flock are barrel-chested and big-footed: they don't take heed,

thirsty for shoots and the dewpond shimmering in the heat.
Her jacket with its too-short-sleeves scratches her arms,
her stockings are wrinkled and hand-me-down boots
scuff clouds of dust along this track from barn to field.

She flicks at a goose with her willow switch. It stretches
its neck and honks at the sun. The flint-faced church
is squatting near the coast. The girl longs for shade,
wants to be nodding in a straight-backed pew,

wedged between her brother and mother.
She imagines the curate's daughter, pale as milk,
lying in a garden wet with bluebells, or swanning
through King's Lynn on market day in a wide-brimmed bonnet.

## x. Well Spring

You were a storm-proof rig when we were bairns,
framed by sunlight. Two brogued feet
planted on the lawn like footings on a sea bed.
Your love was a flaming plume of gas
and when you cradled us, we snoozed
to the lub-dub, lub-dub of your heartbeat.

Then you were diagnosed. Given a few weeks.
We were packed off to an aunt. Skin flaked
from your forearms. You corroded.
Nurses tended a mass of tubes,
careful as mechanics,
calibrating flow. Like the spillage
of the *Torrey Canyon* or *Amoco Cadiz*
the lymphatic truth was seeping out.

# Warming

We loved the blue, that clear space, day after day.
We loved the sunlight, sharpness and heat.
The world was etched on our retinas.

Soon the trees began to shrivel through lack of water.
We dreamt of mackerel skies; of stratus, cirrus—
great banks of fog rolling in from a sea

we could barely remember. We longed for shade, thunder,
for rain in all its forms: the kind that saturated
Gabardines; the kind that drummed on Velux at night;

hail stones to bounce off taut umbrellas that lay unopened
in their stands. Our throats filled up and our pores
were sandpapered with dust. We hung our heads

like goats on a Greek island at the end of summer.
Tongues swelled and language became grunt,
a series of guttural stops. A land gone sour.

We tried to picture our childhoods, when we'd sprawled
on our backs on the moors, created shapes
from clouds: griffins and many-headed beasts
but our children stared—blue and vacant as the sky.

# Fiere

*Scots for companion, friend, equal. (After Jackie Kay)*

And this is what he is to her on cloud-filled days when she swims in the slipstream of her intellect: answers emails, grades portfolios, listens to her students and their Coney-Island, rollercoaster lives. But it's the *fire* in the word that's the catch. Combustible, small things: a lyric from a country song, a modulation to a minor key, her love of Hammond organs, slide guitars and then she's gone into this aching room where all she can do is hold on to the nearest tabletop and burn up, picture his backyard, kissing in the rain. It's these small things:

the sound of a V-twin engine weaving through a traffic jam, a flash of chrome in her wing mirror, or a magazine-spread of Texas photographs and she's strung out like a line of telegraph poles, lost in the beauty of a vanishing point. It's the way he runs the length of a corridor and stands so she can feel his breath on her neck and 'fiere' is *fire, fire, fire.*

# The Winter Solstice

The days can hardly lift themselves and fog
malingers in the silver birch and sulks
the length of dry-stone walls. It wraps the moor
and settles in for weeks—no wind to clear

the air. The sheep are hunkered down, lie waiting
for the year to pivot on the hour.
We're sour as pith. Just when we think we cannot
carry on (the only option seems

to be to slice ourselves in two like lemon
halves), we find a way to stay whole,
to celebrate our juice and yellow zest.
We light the stove: we toast the shortest day

with single malt. The kitchen's bright
and doesn't fill with smoke.

# Blackstone Edge

There was a time on the moor
when you said you loved me and meant it.
Then you turned, climbed into
the work's van and drove back
to Samantha in Milnrow.

I saw you, years later in The Salutation.
We had one of those awkward,
stilted conversations, like two people
standing on a sprung dance floor,
a swimming pool beneath them,

all sealed up and dark;
the smell of chlorine,
other peoples' feet, skin that's shed itself
through endless lengths of front crawl
and morning breast-stroke.

If I could travel back in time
I would argue for love,
state my case for the defence
and grip your arm, pinch
your keys from your leather jacket.

I would reason like a barrister
with my silver-fluted words,
let an ode to Love rise through
the mist, above Blackstone Edge,
tracks of snow across the fields.

My voice would melt reservoir-ice
until water steamed and all the fish boiled white.
The Earth would pause on its axis,
the northern hemisphere feel the full force
of solar winds, the sun's heat.

As the day turned, all the stars would
line up behind Orion and his belt
and give us a standing ovation.
Your poor heart would not
stand a chance.

# Heatwave

The sun burns your shoulders one long afternoon,
your skin is oven-hot. The road
begins to mirage in the heat, the tarmac

bubbles up. We toss and turn all night
beneath a cotton sheet and Yorkshire feels
as if it's set to drift: the county's broken

off and lost its North Sea Fog and Pennine spine.
At some point in the early hours, we come
to rest beside the continental shelf

where Africa is being swallowed by
its dunes. That morning, when we rise, we find
our goldfish upside down and gasping in

his fetid tank. We open all the Velux
and the doors, then circle, ready for a
tiff, a squabble or a full-blown fight

to break this blueness, settled in our lungs.
The news brings no relief as Greece collapses
like a pack of cards, slips further into

debt and massacres take place in Homs,
where fertiliser-workers, dragged from vans,
are lined up by a curb, then shot at point-blank range.

You'd think we'd find a way to pause, to hold
each other, stroke our sunburnt thoughts, but you
begin to peel and cannot bear me near.

We turn our backs and clutch the sweat-soaked
mattress like a raft. We need a flare or thunderstorm
to fill the water butts and clear the moors.

# March

You're kneeling in the borders.
Above your hat, four terracotta pots like coronets.

Snowdrops are sucked mints,
Narcissi shoots spiking the flower beds.

The underside of everything's turned over:
fresh earth, worm casts, spiders' nests.

Water shimmies in the trough
and pirouettes all over your yard.

The bench is too wet to sit on yet.
The broom is bright with yellow buds.

The lavender's wired with dried-up heads
but it's re-sprouting.

You're quick as a vole. Giddy with lengthening
daylight hours as you clip the yew.

The lane winds up the hill—
ribboning the unfenced moors.

# The Glass Heart

I'm full of possibility.
I've been threaded
with a ribbon, wrapped in tissue,
stuffed in the loft for ten months
with fairy lights, a paper angel,
the artificial spruce.

Dust me down, warm me
in the palm of your hand.
I'll remember my genesis:
the glass blower, a furnace,
sand, soda ash, limestone,
my darker Obsidian roots.

Let me be the jar that holds
your morning marmalade,
the mirror in which you brush
your teeth or the coach window
where you rest your cheek
as you head North.

# Lunar Eclipse

The Exe froze over
 and the music of the city was hushed.

You watched
the male swans bunch together

in a moon-shaped space of open water
and held your son close to your chest.

Upstream, Leda let her coat slip
from her shoulders onto snow.

She walked out
                    of her own free will
to meet that feathered rush of air.

You both stared at her, stranded
on the river-ice and drew each other closer.

Above your heads, a wedge of birds
hooted over and over and over.

# The North American Wood Frog

pumps the water from his cells
and fills his body with glucose.
He freezes for the winter:
flat ice crystals form
in his leg muscles, abdomen.
His eyes turn white with frost.

Throughout the blizzards
and short, unlit days,
he remains in stasis.
If he's held
in the cupped palm
of a kind woman

she doesn't have to
possess blue blood.
When the warmth of her kiss
is placed upon his fat,
beautiful face,
he melts to the core.

His heart begins to quicken,
he croaks into life,
leaps into an Alaskan pond
ribboned with spawn.
He stays amphibious
and she's glad of it.

# Skimming

You can never see what's just around
the river bend. Best to let the stone spin
from your palm by chance. Take a little control
by a flex of the knee and a squat stance,
feet planted on wet sand.
Fix your gaze on a midpoint
in the current's still centre. Skim
the flattened oval out with a flick
of the wrist. Live fully for that bounce—
one, two, three across the water like a song:

a trajectory of grace before sinking
into the mud where that old pike lurks,
sensing your every move.

# Raleigh Bikes, 1976

We're freckled, fit as whippets, pedalling up
the narrow road with passing places. Summer
stretches out before us like a quilt.
A farm dog barks, a blackbird scuttles underneath
the privet hedge. We skirt The Edge where
millstone grit butts up against the Cheshire
Moss. We know that days will never be
this clear. Somewhere down below us,

Lindow Man lies flat-faced in the peat,
a noose about his neck, and somewhere up
the ridge, our friend will lose his grip and crack
his skull. For now, we have a den, an oak
to climb, two cans of Sprite. We reach the summit,
turn downhill to face a wall of heat.

# Some Enchanted Evening

I watch the students link arms, queuing under red neon.
An organ's playing deep inside The Picture House.
The projectionist unspools Zeffirelli from rusty cans.
Out on my front step, air is laced with cumin.
Cardamom spits in a neighbour's wok. I light a joint.
*Romeo and Juliet's* about to start.

Ash burns a comet-shaped hole in my skirt.
Although the streets are strewn with chip papers
and greasy polystyrene trays, dusk falls
and Headingley's as lovely as Verona.
All the Kashmiri and Bengali kids on Chopper bikes
lose their appetite for war games and glow like planets.

# Underworld

A barge full of bin-bags
heads out towards the Isle of Dogs:
London flushes itself downstream
as I leg it across Hungerford Bridge.

The Festival Hall is a block of light in the river.
I run past Dreadlocks-Mike, banjo in hand,
nails yellow as vellum, greyhound
hunkered down beside him;

dash by security guards with their
broken-veined cheeks, arms folded
against hoodies skateboarding
the underbelly of the building.

The Camerata tunes to a high G.
I scramble into my uniform behind the till.
The bookshop's crammed with
opera lovers swigging *Bollinger*

spending fifty quid each
on coffee-table art with their Visas.
When Offenbach's *Orpheus*
strikes up, I sneak out to throw coins

in Mike's hat, his greyhound shivering
in a blanket; let the skaters in for a warm
when the guards are off for a fag.
I work a feet-swelling, ten-hour shift,

get the last train home
to Thornton Heath via Brixton.
I have my keys out, ready to stab
any bugger with designs on my handbag.

# Huddersfield General Hospital

A doctor with latex gloves
sawed me in two
like a magician's assistant,
rummaged and pulled something
out by its silken flaps,
whispered reverentially
*Gall bladder... five times its normal size.*

I think of it floating
in formaldehyde
in Caligari's Cabinet.
My wound puckers.
I'm zipped together,
staples zigzagging
like a train track across
the lowlands of my diaphragm.

I press a button for intravenous
morphine. The polystyrene ceiling
fills with balloons: red, yellow,
sky-blue bags of breath.
Patients start to pirouette,
cardigans spangled with sequins.

# Painting the Spiral Staircase

*Thus, though we cannot make our sun*
*stand still, yet we will make him run.*

*Andrew Marvell*

I could lounge in the meadow
'til my skin is stamen-yellow,
listen to the chaffinch on the wire,
calling for its mate, heart about to burst.

I could Hammerite the spiral staircase
in my yard, I could blog or tweet, march
for the women of Afghanistan,
or students on the scrap heap,

plant dahlias in terracotta pots
and marvel at their psychedelic blooms
or choose a younger lover, fuck him silly,
then scrub the sheets.

I could buy a Royal Enfield motorbike,
feel it throbbing on the street.
Time's a gyroscope humming on a string;
a cat out hunting when its dish brims with milk.

# Ageing

Gok Wan would say
I need an overhaul:
should dye my hair roots,
buy a good bra,
force my feet into stilettos,
remember how to flirt.
Then I'd feel young.

But maybe I'll just walk out
of my body altogether,
become air,
a song
a voice
in the silver birch
or fly south with the swifts.

I'll observe the earth-bound
bed in for winter,
the freezing over of thought,
the suspension of love.

# Gold

My goldfish is gasping near the surface of
the murky tank, circling for fish flakes. He
dives between plastic fronds to nose the
gravel. I've had my nose to other peoples'
grindstones all autumn. I rise at four am
and listen to the fish mouthing a language I
can't quite grasp.

Don't get me wrong. There have been clear
moments — my students' smiles when
they've written from the heart, the satisfied
sprawl of my son on the sofa, belly full of
Bolognese. That date with friends: hooting
like owls with laughter, drinking cheap
Cava, pushing the shadow of ageing
parents to the edge of the room so that we
could dance to Abba.

Now I crave a Sunday morning to pay
attention and listen for the fibrillated
creatures of the deep. I need a subterranean
sense of balance; a swim bladder perhaps,
located somewhere in my ribs. Otherwise
I'm that bloody fish with its bent tail —
going round and round, hoping someone
will clean the filter out and let me breathe.

# Sunday Morning, Chichester Cloisters

The ringers take a rest, biceps pulsing with heat
and the weight of the ropes. There's a lull,
full of that call to prayer to a god I no longer believe in.
The silence is bell-shaped and green.

Millions of insects are burrowing
in the oak spreading above my head:
pupating, living and dying in the shade.
A crow squawks. The bell-ringers are ready.

Once lives were measured by chromatic scales
with a stumble in the middle. Now, my Sunday's
punctured by planes stacked up over Gatwick,
a ringtone somewhere in my bag and lines
of metal bodies rocking in the rush hour traffic.

# Seasonal Affective Disorder

is the end of the railroad:
a town where windows are shuttered to snow,
where no one smiles and there's no winter sunrise.

It's a Saab that hates cold weather,
stuttering with a dirty carburettor,
spark plugs losing the will to arc to each other.

By mid-morning it's sliced cheese curling on a plate.
It wraps itself round my guts like wet cloth.
Settles there and spreads.

I need a shift in season, to feel the Saltstraumen
warming with rose fish and halibut,
I need a sea eagle to rid the tundra of vermin.

# Pennine Watershed

Here's the branch where a rope swung:
sent my son orbiting into a rare blue space.
Here are the stones
that mark the burial chambers of his pets —
gerbils, Russian hamsters, fish and newts,
shoe-boxed and tissue-wrapped.

Here's the bridge where I sat down and wept
as my husband packed a rucksack
stuffed with woollen things,
quietly pulled the backdoor shut,
its frame swollen by the winter rains.

I think of the swing and its fraying rope,
cardboard coffins layered with small bones,
the packhorse route: intersecting cobbles
on the steepest slope where a caravan of ponies
puffed to get a purchase on the stone,
clambered up the clough,
across the sphagnum bog to higher ground.

# Gordale Scar

This is our last summer before High School
and the loosening of your day-to-day routine:
I think of how my hours wrap around yours
like hands clasped together in worry
or prayer or something in-between.

You're a lean-limbed goat as we
scramble up the polished path
through a land stripped to the bones
by sheep. Corvids riding the thermals
all day long. Water, limestone, grass.

Here's the Swaledales' black-faced stare,
ewes buttressing their young.
You grimace at a lamb's wrinkled fleece
and umbilical cord shrivelling in the heat.
The beck disappears into the chambers of this earth

and our way ahead is a dry river valley
lined with scree. Mountain ash and hawthorn
cling to the cliffs sculpted by wind.
I take you to the knuckled clints and grykes.
We peer into continents

of herb Robert, wild garlic, Hart's-tongue ferns.
Your freckled cheek is close to mine
but would flame if I kissed you here
in public view. So I kneel close to you
and listen for the water-murmur

beneath our feet, sense the permeable nature
of the rock. The world's in flux.
And you're grinning, content for once
to be by my side, reaching down
to stroke the pin-cushion moss.

# The Handless Maiden

*For Vicki Feaver*

1.

I strap my silver hands on pink stumps
to draw water in the forest,
gather sweet chestnuts,
fold my son close to my chest.

My fingers are engraved
with peacock feathers, knuckles
hinged with golden screws
that catch the early morning light.

I'm full of rage—like a line of fire
burning heather on the moors,
threatening farmsteads, ready to jump
the lanes and swallow every living thing.

2.

I remember Father stood beside me
in the apple orchard, his blade shining,
the Devil at his back.

He placed my thin wrists
on the wood-block. I stared at blossom,
great armfuls that year,

a promise of fruit still to come,
my mouth stuffed with a rag
to stop my screams reaching the village.

Mother dressed each wound, placed
lavender on my pillow to help me sleep.
Didn't utter a word. You bitch, I thought.

Blood oozed through gauze for hours.

3.

Today I feel my phantom fingers ache,
imagine nails, like hopeful moons.

I long to hold a pen,
or pick an apple from a branch

and cup it in my palm.
I sense my fingers bud beneath my skin.

Each tip: rosy and blind.

# Star Swallower

Every time she tried to speak
great beams of light came out.
A beacon amongst women,
her words cut through conversations
like lasers in the night sky
and people knelt before her
to bask in all that iridescence.

At night her body glowed
beneath her quilt like a fridge
with the door ajar. She found it
hard to close her eyes.
She was a sunflower scattering
seeds of light—who longed for
a starless sky, for power cuts,
a coal shed, a cloak
or wartime blackout.

She put her fingers down her throat,
but it was no use. The star was stuck
like a wishbone, scraping
the tissues of her windpipe.
It burnt, leaving her thirsty
for flagons of lemonade,
for mint and honey.

Doctors examined her
but she wrecked the equipment,
short-circuiting everything in sight.
The waiting crowds wanted her pearls
of wisdom, to bask in her language.
She became the starlet of the tabloids:
heaven-sent, a new messiah
who then, like a comet,
disappeared from view.

Some thought she ran away
to Greenland, built an ice-house,
where she sang to herself.
Off the coastline, ships' crews
marvelled at the new aurora borealis.

## Loving the Minotaur

Yew-clipped hedges box me in.
I've no sword, but I cradle this skein
at the entrance, passing it back and forth
over my palms like a question.

The half-man, half-bull I'm looking for is restless,
his coat's matted, his feet cracked
with constant pacing along the gravel paths.
He bellows through the night at the stars—

misunderstood, hunted down, pushed to the mind's
edge. I unspool my wool through
shaded passages and blind alleys, turning this way
and that. I'm near the centre, where I sense

the shifting of his weight from one
flank to the other: he's lowering his horns,
brushing his gold-ringed nose against the stones.
I smell his sweat. He knows I'm here.

# Waymarker

Alice needs a stone dress with a granite skirt and flint buttons,
wants to be rooted on the moors like Churn Milk Joan
pointing to higher ground—above the bogs, water-logged fields,
paths choked with knotweed and balsam.

She needs shoes speckled with mica that catch the light
and warm her feet with the memory of summer
when the hills were hoverfly-drowsy; cattle lounged
on heather roots and chewed the cud, udders rosy with milk.

The days grow short and wet. Her front door begins to stick
and swell. Her lover has migrated to the desert
and the open road. Find her a mallet, a large boulder.
There's no time to lose.

# Shetland

*For Fay Godwin*

Fay did not trek this far north
for evidence of Eden.
Nor was she running from her past.

In 1975 she photographed
a North Sea platform
squatting on the horizon,

pumping out its black gold.
There's a herring gull riding the thermals,
an empty bench in the foreground.

This seat is a block of pure light—
a thought on which to rest,
sprung between wrought-iron struts.

# The Yellow Trousers

*after a painting by Marc Chagall*


A terrier began to howl and a dogs' chorus spread
from barn to barn. All the while, the lovers were caught up
like twine, willing an angel to fly towards St Petersburg,
sing of their love in alleyways and passageways
until the city shimmered like herring.
The girl wriggled free and slipped into the evening.
She could hear her mother calling, calling.

Her young man limped home to a narrow room,
his bed—thin and unwelcoming.
He unzipped his trousers, let his cock slacken
and loll between his thighs like a hound's tongue.
He stood, lighthouse-naked at the window -
watching for a flash of red silk in the pines.
He dreamt of his girl's wrists and their primrose smell.
His trousers were flung over the back of a chair,
holding the shape of his calves long into the night.

# The Marker Stone

*Fay Godwin photograph 1978*

Here's a contoured map
of a whole country laid out before her
from The Orkneys to Kent
peopled with standing stones—
family members who've weathered
squalls with their lichened features.

Dry-stone walls and flooded valleys
slip away from her lens.
There are great open possibilities
of skies and cumulonimbi
building on the curvature of the earth.
She's tilted at an angle, foundations

quaking, the moon sulking low on the hill,
and unnamed beasts brewing
in the mind's blue spaces.

# Slow Train North

You leave King's Cross and lose your mobile signal.
You sit in a tunnel in the Quiet Coach as it rumbles through
the hinterlands of the capital.  Terraced rows give way
to avenues, semis with clipped privet.

You listen to the person opposite breathing to the rhythm
of the diesel engine, and the whirr of the heater.
Your coat's heavy with the weight of it all.
There's your reflection, bunched up like a hare

caught by lamping somewhere in The Wolds.
There's the warmth of your face against glass.
The Wash sprays salt through an open window
and that pull North is stronger than ever.

Maybe you'll cradle ice, rip the skin off your fingertips?
But right now you're reading Louis MacNeice.
This is the *slow movement:* the pause between opening
and closing, the Adagio and Allegro. This is where you are,

between the city and snow, heat and winter.
You're just passing, finding joy in the view:
the wetlands stuffed with trout, rookeries black
with chatter, their fledglings fat with love.

# Baby Snatcher

It was a morning like this when you carried him in–
like Heathcliff, gathered up from a Liverpool slum.
You'd been strange for days, folded our twelve-week
scan into your wallet. You'd taken to following
women with prams, lurking in Mothercare;
stroking babygrows, their velveteen sheen,
kissing small patent shoes, pushing
your thumb into their curves.

But I never thought you'd actually do it,
find the courage to stuff a sleeping form
under your coat, run home, wild-eyed,
in your sheepskin slippers;
never thought I'd find you with milk powder
spattered on the lino, trying to comfort
a Pandora's box of a child - open-mouthed,
yelling blue murder for his mother's nipple.

# Match.com

I was the woman who slipped between hours
of your sons' half-term laughter,
your days spent staring at the Filey coast
through the long lens of your best friend's
broken marriage, watching bracing skies where harriers
rode the thermals and you sighted a rare Scaup.

But when we met, we sat nursing halves
of lager, straight-faced, land-locked.
We stared blankly at Sky Sports in a Bacup pub
full of afternoon gamblers and boozers.

And we will never drink Chablis on my fire escape
or visit Lumb Falls as it freezes into spears of ice.
And you will never kiss my nipples pink
or fold me into your coat, or help me sort
the swifts from swallows on the telephone wire,
looping towards my house as the season warms.

# Ty Newydd

I would like a morning
where I can hum a tune
without a thought in my head,
watch the hawthorn
bent by the sea winds,

feel the companionship
of the voices of this house:
writers who climbed the staircase
with its soft blue carpet,
sat hunched over a desk,

or those servants who slept
in the eaves, tended
Lloyd George's gravel drive,
opened up the sash windows
for a draft of air.

Let me find silence
between the stair-treads,
in dark spice cupboards,
beneath wicker chairs
or secreted in pages

of library books
and in chisel marks of the carving
of a hare and fox.
Let me occupy that calm
when everyone is sleeping
and the tulips are shut mouths.

# Clocks

He wandered through rooms at night with a pair of pliers, wrenching the hands from their clocks. The whole place was suspended and she lost track of the hour, the moon rising like a blank-faced timepiece over the terraces and lines of washing stiff with frost.

When they both thought it was morning, they rose in the dark to scrape ice from the car. The world was bent double as winter approached. 'Don't like change', he said. She nodded, couldn't risk the frozen bridge between them, in case she lost her footing, slipped into black water.

So she humoured him. Hid her diamante-studded wristwatch under her pillow. She let them skate on the surface of their desperate conversations, tried to cook meals at appropriate intervals, hoped that they wouldn't become too nocturnal, wide-eyed, padding about the flat. She stood at the window, stared at the toll route to Keighley: skirting the moor, snaking down into the promise of the valley.

# After Image Two

grief *n* *Leid* *nt* *Kummer* *m* *Gram* *m* *geh*

(because of loss)  große Trauer, Schmerz *m* , Gram *m* *geh*
to cause grief to sb  jdn zutiefst betrüben
[death, loss also]  jdm großen Schmerz bereiten
[failure, sb's behaviour also]  jdm großen Kummer bereiten
to come to grief  Schaden erleiden  (=*be hurt, damaged*)
grief-stricken  adj  untröstlich, tieftraurig
[look, voice]  schmerzerfüllt, gramgebeugt *geh*


## i. Mohrenstrasse

My father's city is full of gaps,
missing buildings,
luggage no longer here.

Today, I find a pathway
resurfaced with granite sets,
a chequer-board of dark and light.

Wealthy Hilton guests
glide in and out
of revolving doors.

Here's the manhole cover
Father photographed,
pungent and oddly sweet,

smelling of the past
that runs beneath me:
wasteland spaces, bombed out squares.

My Father visited in '63
for a sub-committee
of computer programmers,

standardising binary languages.
He spoke fluent Russian,
moved from East to West with ease.

It was the year before I was born.
Mother wore a pink twin-set,
my sister had just turned two.

I look for a lost fountain, Sputnik-shaped,
the trace of a pattern of water
against a slatted fence.

I find fifty-metre cranes,
a cafe selling pomme frites,
Red Bull energy drinks.

Europe unfolds like a
ruffled quilt beneath my feet.
I have not cried in thirty years.

father n (lit, fig) Vater *m* (to sb jdm)


(Old) Father Time     die Zeit (als Allegorie)
fathers *pl* (*=ancestors*) Väter *pl*
(*=founder*) Vater *m*
(*=leader*) Führer *m* , Vater *m liter*
(our) Father     Vater *m* (unser)
 (*=priest*) Pater *m*
birth father         n (*=biological father*) leiblicher Vater
city father         n Stadtverordnete(r) *m*


## ii. Humbolt University

History is tree bark crumbling in my fingers.

Through a zoom lens,
                    I walk into
Father's line of statues silhouetted on the skyline,

Berlin greening itself,
Humbolt and his brother shining white.

Bebelplatz. The site of the Büchverbrennung:

*a librarian sobbing in the vaults*
*of the bibliothek*
*as students and soldiers,*
*high on propaganda,*
*soaked page upon page in petrol*
*to make the paper burn.*

Back in Manchester, the domed library
is a Venetian jewel in the city;
under renovation, with its pale colonnade,
shaded walkway.

There's been a miscalculation.
Not enough shelf space.

Old stock from the vaults is
                    secretly dumped,
junior staff ordered to take trolley
after trolley to the skip;

the writers of the city are up in arms.

A knowledge gap

is a smile with teeth missing,
or a friend's untimely death,
a stolen painting, rectangle
of dust, a hook in the wall.

child n   ( children   *pl* )  (lit, fig)  Kind   *nt*

when I was a child     in or zu meiner Kindheit
flower child     n  Blumenkind   *nt*
latchkey child     n  Schlüsselkind   *nt*
love child     n  außereheliches Kind
problem child     n  Problemkind   *nt*
wild child     n   (Brit)  Wildfang   *m*


## iii. 13th August, 1961

*An apartment block in the city centre.*
*A loud knocking. Two a.m.*
*The Worker's Militia burst in.*
*Gehen! Raus!*
*I watch barbed wire unspooling*
*across our courtyard.*
*Politzei are wearing thick leather gloves.*
*The night is hot and sultry.*

*Neighbours gather*
*in their flannel nightclothes.*
*The sky is grey, washed-out.*
*One family jump from the first floor*
*into the West, holding hands.*
*My husband tries to smoke a roll-up.*
*'Scheisse kerl. Du kannst mich mal.'*
*His lighter won't work.*

wall n  (outside)  *Mauer*  *f*  (inside, of mountain)  Wand  *f*

a wall of fire    eine Feuerwand
a wall of policemen/troops    eine Mauer von Polizisten/Soldaten
walls have ears    die Wände haben Ohren
to come up against a wall of silence    auf eine Mauer des
Schweigens stoßen
to go up the wall    inf  die Wände rauf- or hochgehen *inf*
I'm climbing the walls    inf  ich könnte die Wände hochgehen *inf*
he/his questions drive[s] me up the wall    inf  er/seine Fragerei
bringt mich auf die Palme *inf*


iv. The Reichstag

Father photographed a BRD flag
flying from a tower,
the dome clearly missing.
His viewfinder cut the Brandenburg Gate

straight down the middle.
Technicolor searchlights.
The death strip, the *Todesstreifen,*
red and white barriers

like wounded limbs with their bandages
slipping; a silver car with bevelled
headlights glided to a halt
at a checkpoint that cut

the street in two. A stretch of concrete
runs through his picture, slightly blurred.
I think this is The Wall.
Study the Kodachrome more closely and I'm sure.

Today, you cannot see the Reichstag
from where my dad stood with his shaking hands.
Embassies in Pariserplatz block the view.
Two fountains rise and fall,

a musician plays a flute,
tourists pose
in ones and twos
with actors in Russian uniforms.

One street entertainer
is dressed as Darth Vader,
another sweats
inside a Berlin bear suit.

memory   n  Gedächtnis   *nt*

(=*faculty*)  Erinnerungsvermögen   *nt*
from memory     aus dem Kopf
to lose one's memory     sein Gedächtnis verlieren
to commit sth to memory     sich ( *dat* ) etw einprägen
[poem]  etw auswendig lernen
to have a long memory     ein langes Gedächtnis haben
I have a bad memory for faces/names     ich habe ein schlechtes
Personengedächtnis/Namensgedächtnis
he had happy memories of his father     er verband angenehme
Erinnerungen mit seinem Vater


## v. The Fall, 1989

East Berliners stream through checkpoints:
*Claus, Anton, Maria who bist du?*
People are hugging complete strangers.

They force open a gate,
push through the striped barriers.
Guards try fire hoses, but soon give up.

One couple light up sparklers
and fire-write their names
into the velvet blackness.

Students from both sides
link hands and dance,
then clamber all over the wall itself.

The night is fur-lined with love,
resplendent with cheers
and singing and clapping

and people with streaked faces,
elastic with delight.
Someone attacks concrete

with a sledgehammer.
Everyone is testing just how far
freedom will stretch.

Soldier n Soldat(in)   *m(f)*

soldier of fortune   Söldner(in)   *m(f)*
old soldier   altgedienter Soldat   (fig)   alter Kämpe
old soldiers never die, (they just fade away)   (prov)   manche
Leute sind nicht totzukriegen *inf*
(Zool) Soldat   *m*
 vi   Soldat(in) sein, (in der Armee) dienen
tired of soldiering   des Soldatenlebens müde
soldier on   vi   unermüdlich weitermachen
two of them soldiered on to the top   zwei kämpften sich bis
zum Gipfel vor
tin soldier   n   Zinnsoldat   *m*


## vi. Russian War Cemetery, Treptower Park

Ten to eight. The sun is low,
casting shadows over English-speaking punks
drinking *Amstel* below me on the steps.

I watch light catch a line of poplars,
the wind humming
like an old soldier through their leaves.

I'm very tired. Stand in my father's footsteps,
for the final time, next to a Red Army Guard
on bended knee, cast in bronze.

Someone's tied a red ribbon
round his rifle. Jurassic limestone
shades the well-trimmed lawns.

When I was eleven, my father's ashes
were scattered on a rose bush.
No gravestone.

Today, a couple chat in Russian: the woman
dressed from head to toe in leopard print
with flowers in her hands.

Soon the sun will set,
pink granite start to glitter
in the dying light.

This trip's nearly over. I'll pack away
my father's prints. Go home
and cook dinner for my son,

teach my students how to write
a sonnet, repoint the house
before winter.